HIGHLANDS OF
SCOTLAND

Colin Baxter Photography, Grantown-on-Spey, Scotland

HIGHLANDS OF SCOTLAND

The image of the Highlands has often suffered from the over-romanticism of writers, artists and film-makers alike. Too often it has been the superficial 'shortbread and tartan' which has been emphasized over the true culture and history of the place. The Highlands neither need nor deserve that sort of romantic role; they offer much more in their reality than any of the fictitious idealism.

The sense of place evoked by the Highlands is profound. It has been captured here in this collection which not only preserves instants in time but also alludes to moments in history: each castle has a long story to tell; each town and village is the physical consequence of long human endeavour; and events like the Braemar Highland Gathering, so recent in its origin, are nevertheless based on ancient rites and ceremonies drawn from clan society.

Of course, there is the landscape to consider. It ranges from high cliffs and sandy beaches to long-fingered lochs, and from green pastures and cultivated ground to moor and mountain sides. Above it all rise the summits of the mountains themselves which give the Highlands their name.

Though a relatively small area, the landscape of Highland Scotland is truly magnificent. It is grand, it is fragile and it is at times unbelievably beautiful. For all their variety and for the breadth of their history, the Highlands hold a special place in the minds of people all over the world.

Loch Katrine, Trossachs

At the very heart of Rob Roy country, the beauty of Loch Katrine has inspired writers and poets alike; it is the 'lake' around which Walter Scott wrote *The Lady of the Lake*.

◀ Loch Lomond from the air

Loch Lomond is the largest freshwater expanse in Scotland, and its 'bonnie banks' are famously commemorated in song. The tree-covered islands of Inchcailloch and Clairinsh stand in the foreground here, while Ben Lomond, top right in the distance, is the most southerly of Scotland's Munros (mountains over 3000 ft/914 m high).

CASTLE STALKER, APPIN, ARGYLL

The precise lines of Castle Stalker rise clear above the Rock of the Cormorants in
Loch Linnhe. A classic tower house built for the Stewart king, James IV, about 1540,
it changed hands many times with the turbulent fortunes of the Stewarts in Appin.

KILCHURN CASTLE AND LOCH AWE, ARGYLL ▶

The massive tower house of Kilchurn Castle, a stronghold of the Campbells,
was built around 1440. It stands at the north-eastern end of Loch Awe,
which at a length of around 24 miles (39 km) is Scotland's longest loch.

◀ BEN CRUACHAN AND LOCH ETIVE, ARGYLL

The low sun of an autumn day lights the rounded contours of the seven-peaked Ben Cruachan above the calm waters of Loch Etive. A peaceful scene which belies the name of Etive itself, from the Gaelic for 'raging', and also, the constant sound of turbines deep inside the mountain. These generators produce electricity from the power of the mountain's water which was first dammed in a high corrie in 1965 at the start of the Loch Awe Hydro-Electric Scheme, south of Loch Etive.

FALLS OF DOCHART, KILLIN, PERTHSHIRE

The tumbling cascade is named from the Gaelic for 'scouring water'. A magical place associated with folklore and fairy-tales, wicked chieftains and clan battles; a small standing stone marks the burial place of the mighty giant warrior Fingal. At nearby Finlarig Castle there is the only surviving beheading pit in Scotland.

GLENCOE

From high on Am Bodach the floor of this famous 11 mile (18 km) glen is clearly defined. The River Coe cuts through the green pasture where once the valley was scoured by ice and water. Towering above are Bidean nam Bian and Aonach Dubh.

BEN NEVIS FROM THE NORTH-WEST

The highest mountain in Britain. Although 4406 ft (1343 m) 'the Ben' does
not emerge from the surrounding plateau as a resplendent summit, yet beneath
its rounded mass is one of the most challenging rock climbs in the country.

ABOVE BEN MORE, NEAR CRIANLARICH, PERTHSHIRE

The dramatic forms of the central and northern Highlands of Scotland owe their existence to the profound geological processes of folding, deposition, intrusion and erosion. The hills pictured above are substantially made of ancient metamorphic rocks, folded by heat and pressure, then sculpted by glacial ice before being overlain by younger sedimentary layers. In the distance on the right, Ben Nevis rises just above the rest.

RED DEER STAG ►

The majestic red deer stag stands proud as Scotland's largest native animal, and was immortalised by Landseer in his famous painting the 'Monarch of the Glen'. But to reign supreme a stag must first be victorious in battles of the autumn rut, when he then gains overlordship of a group of hinds for a short time.

The red deer evolved as a woodland species, but with the devastation of the Highland forests they were forced to the open moorlands, the treeless 'deer forests' of today. Big animals, sometimes reaching 300 lb (140 kg), they impact heavily on their habitat. Without natural predators such as wolves, deer stalking is the only real control on the ever-growing red deer population, although foxes and eagles may kill a few calves each year.

◀ LOCHNAGAR AND
   BALMORAL CASTLE,
   ROYAL DEESIDE

The white granite of
Balmoral Castle glints
amid the autumn colours
of Deeside beneath the
dark slopes of Lochnagar.
A favourite royal residence
since it was built and
furnished to Prince Albert's
design in 1855, two years
after he and Queen Victoria
bought the estate. In contrast
to the northern and western
Highlands the contours
of Deeside are gentle, the
landforms smoothed by
broad-leaved trees and
productive farmlands.

BRAEMAR HIGHLAND GAMES
– THE MASSED PIPES AND DRUMS

Today the Braemar Highland Games are known worldwide.
The event is now altered beyond recognition from its
beginnings as a charity walk for local carpenters. Competitive
'games' were first introduced in the 19th century but it was
with the patronage of Queen Victoria, after she purchased
nearby Balmoral, that the Braemar Gathering and other
Highland Games really prospered.

◄ THE CAIRNGORM MOUNTAINS
FROM THE AIR

The Cairngorm plateau is Britain's
highest mountain range. Vast and
desolate, it is broken by four peaks of
over 4000 ft/1219 m. While part of its
northern corries is a popular skiing area,
it is for their massive form, rich flora and
fauna and sub-arctic habitat that these
ancient mountains are truly renowned.

LOCH PITYOULISH, ►
STRATHSPEY

Reflections in the tranquil waters of Loch
Pityoulish. The woodlands in this area are
almost unique to Strathspey. A mosaic
of Scots pine, silver birch, rowan, juniper
and bilberry, these pinewoods differ little
from those which clothed much of the
Highlands at the end of the last Ice Age.

URQUHART CASTLE AND LOCH NESS

Standing on a promontory overlooking the world-famous loch, Urquhart Castle was once one of the largest castles in Scotland. On an historic site used since at least the Iron Age, Urquhart was developed as an important royal fortress from about 1200.

THE RIVER NESS AND LOCH NESS FROM THE NORTH ▶

Eilean Donan Castle and Loch Duich

Scotland's most photographed castle stands on an ancient and strategic site where the waters of three sea lochs meet. Clan seat of the Macraes, the present castle was rebuilt between 1912 and 1932 when the arched bridge was added to join it to the mainland.

◀ The Five Sisters of Kintail and Loch Duich

The waters of Loch Duich draw a sharp line below the jagged peaks of the Five Sisters, all part of the inhospitable territory of the Clan Mackenzie, to whom the Clan Macrae provided armed protection and became known as 'the Mackenzies' coat of mail'.

SCONSER POST OFFICE, ISLE OF SKYE

For so many places in the Highlands the local sub-post office is at the hub of the community. Every kind of building has been used for the purpose, like this one with its once typical corrugated iron roof. A short boat journey from here is the island of Raasay where Bonnie Prince Charlie once swore to replace the turf houses with 'proper' stone ones.

THE ISLE OF SKYE ▶ ACROSS THE INNER SOUND

On the horizon in this evening view, from the road between Applecross and Loch Kishorn, the Cuillin mountains are softened by purple hues, but these are some of the most formidable mountains in Britain.

The jagged gabbro peaks of the Black Cuillins are eroded now to narrow ridges and pinnacles; distant imaginings to all but the most skilful climbers. Their name may have been given by Norse men who saw them from afar as *kjollen* or keel-shaped.

BEINN EIGHE AND LOCH COULIN, WESTER ROSS

Beinn Eighe became Britain's first National Nature Reserve in 1951.
Its unique flora and fauna are protected and encouraged by deer and sheep control.
But, it is still best-known for its massive geological forms and scree slopes.

◄ THE TORRIDON HILLS ACROSS LOCH EWE, WESTER ROSS

Sometimes described as Scotland's last wilderness, the red sandstone mountains of
Torridon are the result of unimaginable geological upheaval some 800 million years ago.

INVERPOLLY NATIONAL NATURE RESERVE FROM THE SUMMIT OF SUILVEN

An eternal landscape formed by a vast plain of gneiss. But this is not a desolate place;
it is home to a wealth of bird, animal and plant life now protected in the Reserve.

ULLAPOOL AND LOCH BROOM, WESTER ROSS ▶

Two hundred and fifty years ago Loch Broom was alive with shoals of herring
but there was no harbour where fish could be landed. It was not until 1792 that
the British Fisheries Society planned and built the fishing village of Ullapool.

◄ OLDSHOREMORE, SUTHERLAND

Like many crofting villages, Oldshoremore was forced into existence about 200 years ago during the Highland Clearances, as people were cleared from the better land to make way for sheep, or because of population pressure and famine. And here, scattered along the coastal strip, people still make a living where the plant life is stunted by the unforgiving wind; trees and bushes are small and bent and few wild flowers are brave enough to stretch beyond a few inches from the peaty ground.

ARDVRECK CASTLE, LOCH ASSYNT, SUTHERLAND

The crumbling ruin of this 15th-century tower house was once a MacLeod stronghold. Most famously, it was for a short time, a prison to James Graham Marquis of Montrose following his defeat at Carbisdale in 1650; from here he was taken south to die on the gallows in Edinburgh.

DUNNET BAY FROM THE AIR, CAITHNESS

Dunnet Head in the distance is the most northerly
point on the Scottish mainland (not John o' Groats as
is popularly thought). The tip of the headland is crowned
with a Victorian lighthouse which towers above remarkable
cliffs, haunt of many seabirds. On the horizon is Hoy, one
of the Orkney Islands.

BEN LOYAL AND ▶ KYLE OF TONGUE, SUTHERLAND

The shimmering waters of
the Kyle of Tongue, watched
over by the heights of Ben
Loyal, seem an unlikely stage
for events of major historical
import. Yet it was here that
the fate of Bonnie Prince
Charlie's Jacobite uprising
of 1745 was most probably
sealed, when an English
frigate forced aground a sloop
carrying gold from the French
king for the Prince's cause.
The crew tried to carry the
gold south but were easily
caught and defeated by
the local clan Mackay.

GLENFINNAN VIADUCT, WEST HIGHLAND LINE

This monument to railway engineering cuts across Glen Finnan,
carrying the West Highland railway line between Fort William and Mallaig.
This section of the line was opened in 1901.

Published in Great Britain in 2000 by Colin Baxter Photography Ltd,
Grantown-on-Spey, Moray PH26 3NA, Scotland

Text by Lorna Ewan

Photographs & Text Copyright © Colin Baxter 2000   All rights reserved.

A CIP Catalogue record for this book is available from the British Library.

ISBN 1-84107-052-1   *Colin Baxter Gift Book Series*   Printed in Hong Kong

Page one photograph: **Creag Meagaidh**   Page two photograph: **Glen Barrisdale & Loch Hourn, Knoydart**
Front cover photograph: **The Cairngorms & Loch an Eilein**   Back cover photograph: **Loch Kanaird, Wester Ross**